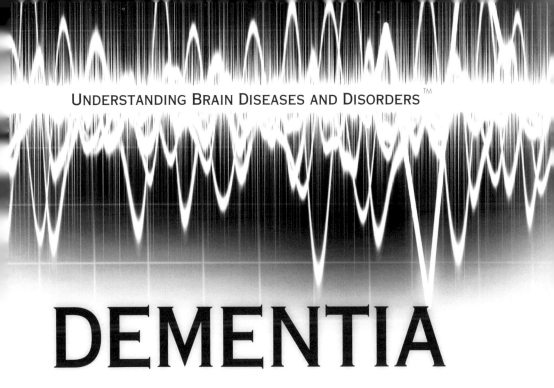

UNDERSTANDING BRAIN DISEASES AND DISORDERS™

DEMENTIA

THERESE SHEA

D1606734

ROSEN
PUBLISHING®

New York

Published in 2012 by The Rosen Publishing Group, Inc.
29 East 21st Street, New York, NY 10010

Copyright © 2012 by The Rosen Publishing Group, Inc.

First Edition

Library of Congress Cataloging-in-Publication Data

Shea, Therese.
Dementia/Therese Shea.—1st ed.
     p. cm.—(Understanding brain diseases and disorders)
Includes bibliographical references and index.
ISBN 978-1-4488-5545-2 (library binding)
1. Dementia—Juvenile literature. I. Title.
RC521.S43 2012
616.8'3—dc23

                                                          2011015653

Manufactured in China

CPSIA Compliance Information: Batch #W12YA: For further information, contact Rosen Publishing, New York, New York, at 1-800-237-9932.

CONTENTS

4...Introduction

Chapter 1
The Cerebrum, Memory, and Dementia...6

Chapter 2
13...The Many Signs of Dementia

Chapter 3
The Many Causes of Dementia...21

Chapter 4
32...The Diagnosis

Chapter 5
Treating Progressive Dementia...41

Chapter 6
48...Palliative Care

Glossary...55

57...For More Information

For Further Reading...60

62...Index

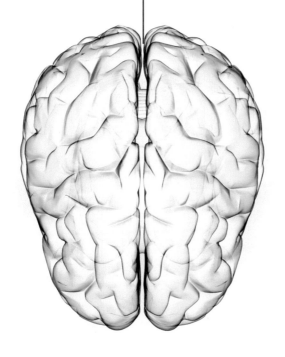

Introduction

The human brain is a delicate mass of nerve tissue protected by the skull. The brain has one hundred billion nerve cells, or neurons. Each neuron processes, stores, and transmits information to other neurons using chemicals called neurotransmitters. Neurons working together form networks of communication. Some networks are dedicated to learning, others to remembering, still others to movement, and so on.

Though the human brain can now be tested, scanned, and analyzed in many ways without harm, there are still many mysteries about how it works. What is not a mystery is the fragile nature of this organ. The connections between neurons need large amounts of energy and oxygen to work successfully. People can partially control this by adopting a healthy diet and lifestyle. However, some conditions are not in one's control.

The brain slowly loses some of its abilities as we grow older. It's difficult to predict how aging will affect our behavior and cognitive abilities.

Brain injury can occur in many ways: aging, genetic diseases, infections, trauma, tumors, strokes, nutritional deficiencies, diseases such as Alzheimer's, and many more. Some injuries and disorders in the brain result in outward symptoms that are labeled as dementia. Memory and cognitive decline are the most often associated symptoms, while changes in personality and behavior may also occur. Dementia can have devastating effects. However, it is possible that the symptoms can be slowed, halted, or even reversed. In recent years, with the steady increase of people being diagnosed with dementia, research is focusing on early detection and more effective treatments of related brain disorders.

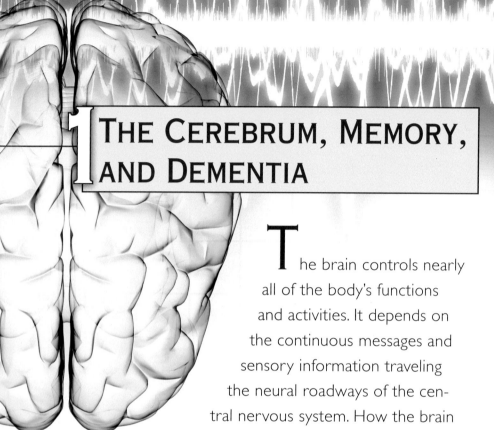

1 THE CEREBRUM, MEMORY, AND DEMENTIA

The brain controls nearly all of the body's functions and activities. It depends on the continuous messages and sensory information traveling the neural roadways of the central nervous system. How the brain responds to these signals and performs tasks is unique to each individual. Our brains make us who we are—how we think, how we act, and how we feel. Despite the many mysteries surrounding the brain, neurologists have developed an understanding of the brain's "map." They know the locations in the brain where many of the body's functions are controlled. The map of the cerebrum is especially important to those who study the effects of dementia on the brain, as many of the disorders and diseases that cause dementia attack the cerebrum first.

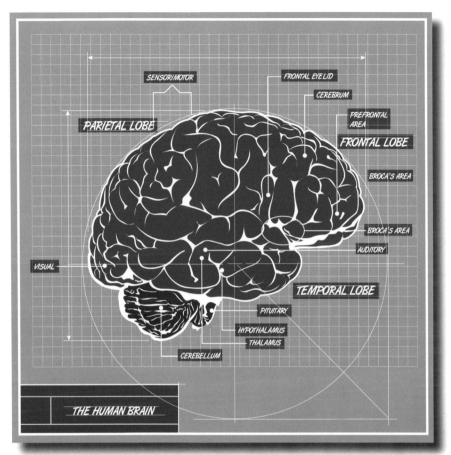

SENSORIMOTOR

FRONTAL EYE LID

CEREBRUM

PREFRONTAL AREA

PARIETAL LOBE

FRONTAL LOBE

BROCA'S AREA

BROCA'S AREA

AUDITORY

VISUAL

TEMPORAL LOBE

PITUITARY

HYPOTHALAMUS

THALAMUS

CEREBELLUM

THE HUMAN BRAIN

Although scientists know which parts of the brain are primarily responsible for certain functions, they also acknowledge that there is much to be learned about the brain's capabilities.

Mapping the Cerebrum

The wrinkly outer surface of the cerebrum is called the cerebral cortex. It is the part of the cerebrum that's divided in two by a deep crevice running from front to back. Each half is divided into parts called lobes. The frontal lobe is located just behind the forehead. It is the control center of our personality. The frontal lobe is also involved in fine motor skills, problem solving, memory, language, judgment, spatial orientation, and social behaviors. Unfortunately, the frontal lobe's location puts it at risk for injury. Injuries can affect some or all of its functions.

The lobe located behind the frontal lobe is the parietal lobe, which receives information from different senses. Touch and pain neural processes are centered there, as well as the audio and visual information needed to understand language.

The temporal lobe is found behind the temples, which are the sides of the head behind the eyes. This lobe has a large role in memory, hearing, speech, and behavior.

In the rearmost part of the cerebrum is the occipital lobe. Also called the visual cortex, the occipital lobe is the part of the brain most responsible for vision.

Under the cerebral cortex are components of the limbic system: the hypothalamus, the amygdala, and the hippocampus. The hypothalamus has a hand in eating, sleeping, body temperature, and hormone regulation. The amygdala is a center of emotion, especially fear and anger, and is associated with visual learning and memory. The hippocampus is the memory organizer. It processes information and sends it to the cerebral cortex to be stored as memory. When the information needs to be accessed again, the hippocampus recalls it.

The Gray Matter

The part of the brain that is responsible for intellect is sometimes referred to as the "gray matter." This nickname comes from the color of the cerebral cortex when removed from the body. It is gray or gray-ish brown, while the rest of the brain is white. The color difference occurs because the cortex is exposed in its position on the exterior, while the other parts of the brain are insulated. The cerebral cortex is the top portion of the cerebrum and is only about .2 inch (.5 centi-meter) thick. Though the cortex is thin, its wrinkles and folds add to its surface area.

Many of the tasks and functions attributed to these lobes are collaborative efforts with other parts of the brain. Indeed, no map of the brain can offer a complete picture of its interconnectedness.

Making Memories

Short-term memories—those we can recall immediately, but for a limited time—are supported by both the frontal and pari-etal lobes. Short-term memories can be reinforced by repeated use, in which case the hippocampus plays a role in storing them as long-term memories. For example, if a person reads the words of a song, he or she will remember many of those words immediately after the song sheet is taken away. However, if the words for the song are never read or heard again, most likely

Frequently examining photographs can help sustain a person's long-term memories about people and events, keeping dementia at bay.

the song will soon be forgotten. If the words are reread repeatedly with the learner closely paying attention, the lyrics will be committed to long-term memory and thus will be less easily forgotten.

Another way information is registered into long-term memory is through association with traumatic events. For example, many people remember where they were and what they were doing when they heard about the attacks on the World Trade Center on September 11, 2001. Memories are stored in specific parts of the cerebral cortex depending on their nature. A memory of a sound, such as a bird's tweet, is stored in the temporal lobe, which contains the auditory area of the brain. The memory of what a rose or garlic smells like is stored in the parietal lobe. Some memories involve multiple senses. Perhaps the smell of cookies reminds someone of their grandmother's apartment. Memories are complex, as is the brain's role in maintaining them.

The Three Major Parts of the Brain

Billions of neurons make up the three major parts of the human brain: the brain stem, the cerebellum, and the cerebrum.

The brain stem is located in the hindbrain, where the spinal cord meets the brain. It controls involuntary, automatic functions of the human body, such as the heartbeat and breathing. The brain stem also transmits messages from the spinal cord (which carries nerve signals to and from the rest of the body) to other parts of the brain. The brain and spinal cord make up the central nervous system.

The cerebellum is located in the back and underside of the brain. It is the center of coordination and balance, and it is involved with the voluntary movement of legs and arms. It is the largest part of the human brain. The outer surface of the cerebellum is the wrinkled, folded portion of the brain seen in pictures.

The cerebrum is responsible for the most complex functions of the brain. When looked at from above, the cerebrum is separated from front to back by a groove. Each side of the cerebrum controls skilled movement for the opposite side of the body. The cerebrum is also the center of functions associated with intelligence, such as reasoning, organizing, decision making, and creating. It receives and processes information from the senses. The cerebrum is also vital for memory storage, language comprehension, and spatial recognition.

This image illustrates the transmitting of information from one neuron to another. Neurotransmitters cross the gap between the neurons, called a synapse.

Neurodegeneration

As people age, their brains become less efficient. It is a natural process for neurons to die every day, even in the healthiest individuals. By the time we are older, some of the functions of the brain are less efficient, such as memory making and accessing. Becoming forgetful is a natural part of aging. However, the natural progression of an aging brain should not stop someone from living a full life. When it does, the warning signs of dementia signal a serious problem.

Dementia doesn't mean forgetfulness, and it doesn't mean "being crazy." Dementia is not a brain disorder itself but is the sign of a disorder, disease, or multiple afflictions. When cognitive functions, such as memory, become severely impaired, a neurodegenerative disorder is often the cause. Though the reasons for the onset of many disorders are a mystery, recent technology can sometimes detect their presence, even in the early stages. Some causes of neurodegeneration can be treated successfully, even prevented, if identified early enough.

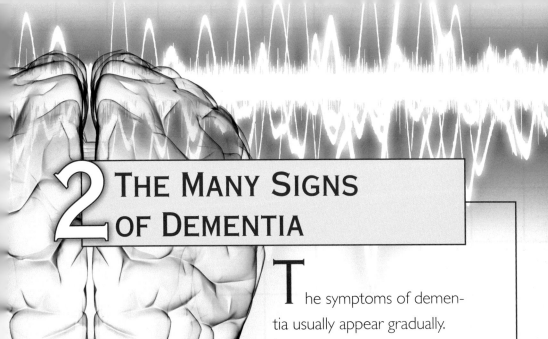

2 THE MANY SIGNS OF DEMENTIA

The symptoms of dementia usually appear gradually. The affected person is most often the first to notice a change, especially if it upsets his or her daily routine like memory loss does. Other indications of dementia, such as personality differences, may be more apparent to others. Dementia reveals itself as some or all of the following symptoms: memory loss, executive dysfunction, spatial disorientation, personality and behavior changes, communication difficulties, and physical and psychological effects.

Memory Loss

The most common symptom linked with dementia is memory loss. At first, it may be difficult to tell the difference between normal age-related memory loss and dementia, especially in older people. In memory loss associated with old age, a person may forget a birthday. He or she may fail to remember a name.

Though dementia may begin like this, it is progressive, meaning symptoms worsen over time. Instead of merely forgetting to show up for an appointment on Tuesday, the afflicted person may not know it is Tuesday or that he or she even had an appointment. In addition, if prompted to remember, a person with severe dementia may not retain the information. Short-term memory is frequently affected. Other signs of dementia-generated memory loss are misplacing objects and repeating conversations. An inability to keep track of time is also a symptom.

Executive Dysfunction

The inability to reason, organize, or work toward a goal is sometimes labeled as executive dysfunction. Simply put, this is the failure to execute a task, and it is another sign of dementia. Everyday easy-to-handle problems, such as using money or cooking, become overwhelming. Often, the patient gets stuck on a single step or detail of the task and cannot reason around the obstacle.

If the person experiencing executive dysfunction is still in the working world, he or she may mishandle everyday tasks. Multitasking, or doing more than one task at a time, becomes nearly impossible. This affects activities such as driving a car. Severe executive dysfunction makes it dangerous for a dementia sufferer to live without a full-time caregiver.

Spatial Disorientation

Spatial disorientation is the inability to figure out where one is. Without this ability, a person becomes confused about his or her whereabouts and cannot determine a direction to get where he or she wants to go. A dementia sufferer can lose the ability to recognize familiar roads, routes, and landmarks.

To those with dementia, they haven't changed—the outside world has. They may get lost walking on a path they have traveled hundreds of times. Some people who are severely affected by dementia even lose their way in their own homes. The desire to wander is a behavioral change that may accompany spatial disorientation, making the problem worse. The more the dementia progresses, the more spatial disorientation puts the patient in danger, even more so when coupled with memory loss.

Memory loss can make spatial disorientation even more devastating to dementia sufferers, hindering their ability to correct their mistakes.

Personality and Behavior Changes

With their world seemingly changed so much, anxiety, fear, and paranoia often become a major part of dementia patients' personalities. However, changes in personality do not always stem from a reason. A person with a gentle nature may turn violent unexpectedly. A happy person can become gloomy. Sometimes personalities are volatile, changing moods from one moment to the next. A small event may upset a person with dementia. A task that he or she cannot remember how to perform, such as tying shoes, may cause the person to become agitated, angry, or depressed.

The frontal and temporal lobes of the brain are the center of a person's judgment and behavior. When certain diseases and disorders attack these areas, behavioral changes result. A dementia sufferer may say inappropriate comments or act in surprising ways, such as refusing to clean. In some cases, a person with dementia may suffer from hallucinations.

Communication Difficulties

Dementia may develop into difficulties in communicating, signaling neurodegeneration in the parietal and frontal lobes. These problems can range from searching for the right word to using a word that sounds similar to the correct word. They may settle for defining the word they mean: "that thing that makes

Depression is a common sign of dementia. Fortunately, it's often a treatable symptom. With the right therapy and possible medication, depression sufferers can resist feelings of hopelessness.

teeth clean" substitutes for "toothbrush." The ability to construct a sentence is reduced to a few words.

Understanding others can also be a problem. Background noises in particular are confusing; the patient may not distinguish what is being said from surrounding sounds. Memory loss can make things worse if the person is unable to remember what he or she hears long enough to process the meaning. Sometimes the dementia patient cannot understand written words if the connection between words and their meanings is severed.

Forgetfulness vs. Dementia

Everyone can be forgetful. As people age, forgetfulness becomes more frequent. However, there is no cause for panic—it is not necessarily a sign that dementia is the problem. Here are some examples of differences between those who are merely forgetful versus those with progressive dementia:

Forgetfulness	Dementia
Misplaces keys	Can't remember what keys are used for
Forgets a birthday	Doesn't know the day of the week
Jokes about forgetting	Isn't aware of forgetfulness
Forgets a person's name for a moment	Has no memory of a person they know well

However, if there is any question or concern, get checked out by a professional.

Physical and Psychological Effects

All of the symptoms mentioned so far focus on the brain, but dementia also has an effect on other parts of the body, both directly and indirectly. Memory loss can cause problems for people who need to maintain their health through medication.

Either not remembering to take medicine—or "remembering" several times and taking multiple doses—can result in an emergency situation. Another effect of memory loss is an inability to remember personal hygiene, the most basic way of keeping oneself healthy.

Simply remembering to eat can be problematic for people with dementia. They may lose the ability to tell the difference between what is edible and what is not edible. Malnutrition and dehydration are common in dementia patients and can lead to other health problems.

Memory loss and cognitive decline hinder dementia sufferers' ability to maintain their health, especially if they're taking prescription medicine. The aid of a caregiver becomes even more important.

Dementia may affect the parts of the brain that control coordination. The loss of coordination is called apraxia. It is demonstrated in unsteady walking and an inability to use tools easily. Apraxia impacts many parts of an active person's life, from driving to using a fork and, more severely, chewing and swallowing food.

Dementia has a major impact on the emotional life of the dementia patient. Anger, confusion, anxiety, and depression are common reactions to diagnosis and to the changes in the patient's life. Depression, in particular, may lead to symptoms progressing as common side effects of poor nutrition and difficulty sleeping weaken the body.

The many symptoms and effects of dementia will not all be present in a single patient. Doctors have found that specific symptoms correlate to the disorder or disorders that are attacking the brain and causing the dementia.

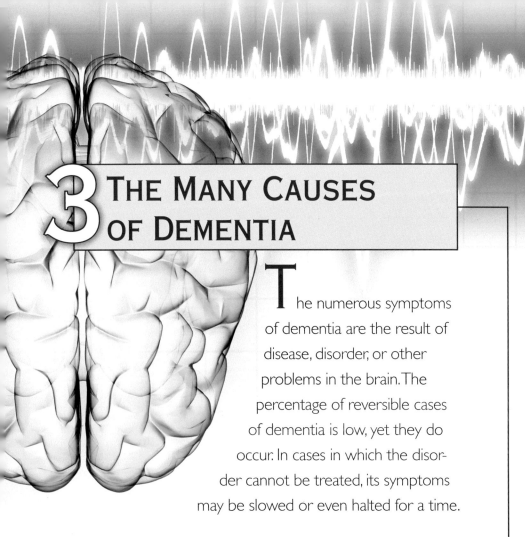

3 THE MANY CAUSES OF DEMENTIA

The numerous symptoms of dementia are the result of disease, disorder, or other problems in the brain. The percentage of reversible cases of dementia is low, yet they do occur. In cases in which the disorder cannot be treated, its symptoms may be slowed or even halted for a time.

Treatable Causes of Dementia

The treatable (or sometimes partially treatable) causes of dementia include various kinds of infections. In these cases, the suddenness of the dementia hints at the cause. As the body's immune system fights an infection, it uses a response such as fever. The swelling that may result around the brain can disrupt neural processes, bringing on dementia. Encephalitis and meningitis are two serious infections that target the brain and its surrounding membrane; confusion and memory loss may follow. Similarly, leukemia and multiple sclerosis—though not infections—affect the body's immune system and can result in dementia as well.

Dementia may also stem from abnormalities in the endocrine system. This is the system of glands and hormones that work to regulate many of the body's functions. Low thyroid hormone levels in the blood, called hypothyroidism, slow the body's chemical reactions. These include metabolic processes that convert fuel from foods into energy for the brain. If that process fails, forgetfulness and loss of concentration result. Hypoglycemia is the deficiency of sugar (or glucose) in the bloodstream. A long-term effect of depriving the brain of glucose is dementia later in life.

Dementia can be a consequence of nutritional deficiencies, too. B vitamins, in particular, aid in cognitive functions. Alcoholics often lack vitamin B1, damaging their short-term memory. People with an inability to absorb vitamin B12 may experience personality changes and depression. Severe deficiency of vitamin B6 can also cause dementia. Calcium, a role-player in the transmission of messages between neurons, is another necessary part of the diet. In addition, too little or too much sodium in the bloodstream can alter brain function as dehydration does.

Sometimes a medication or interacting medications lead to reactions or side effects that mimic dementia. Dementia can also originate from exposure to lead or other poisonous substances. People with alcohol and drug addictions may display signs of dementia even after the substance abuse has ended. In these cases, symptoms may not go away after treatment, depending on how badly the brain is damaged.

The brain requires a high level of oxygen to function. Heart attacks, asthma, smoke or carbon monoxide inhalation, extremely high altitude, strangulation, and anesthesia overdose can all diminish the brain's oxygen supply. Problems such as lung disease and heart disease, which prevent the brain from receiving adequate oxygen, can starve brain cells and cause dementia.

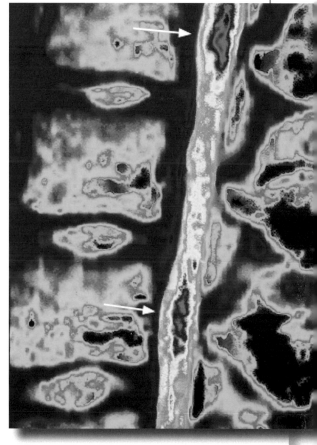

The red and pink areas on the spinal cord represent neural damage associated with multiple sclerosis. When dementia results, the disease is labeled cerebral multiple sclerosis.

The likely result of a head injury, a subdural hematoma is bleeding between the brain's surface and its outer covering. This mass of blood can exert pressure on neurons, bringing on dementia. Though rare, brain tumors can also cause dementia. Symptoms include changes in personality or problems with speech, language, thinking, and memory.

Causes of Progressive Dementia

Doctors who have ruled out the treatable causes of dementia—or treated them without signs of dementia diminishing—look next to irreversible brain disorders. The dementias stemming from these disorders and diseases worsen progressively, especially without medical intervention.

Alzheimer's Disease

Alzheimer's disease is the most common disorder that causes dementia. In fact, the two terms are often used interchangeably. According to Robert Levine's *Defying Dementia: Understanding and Preventing Alzheimer's and Related Disorders*, an estimated 50 to 75 percent of all cases of dementia are caused by Alzheimer's disease alone or in connection with another brain disorder. More than four million people in the United States suffer from Alzheimer's, and over twenty million worldwide. These numbers are expected to more than double by the year 2050.

Careful studies of Alzheimer's disease, especially in recent years, have provided a glimpse into the destructive nature of dementia. Scientists think Alzheimer's disease prevents neurons from connecting with each other. As the neurons lose the ability to do their jobs, they die. As they die, dysfunction manifests itself.

Alzheimer's patients have an abnormal amount of beta-amyloid proteins in their brains. These proteins form abnormal deposits within the brain. These proteins are divided into two types: plaques, which are buildups between neurons, and tangles, which are twisted within neurons. How these plaques and tangles kill nerve cells isn't understood, only that their presence is damaging.

The most common early symptom of Alzheimer's is difficulty remembering new information. This indicator is consistent with the finding that beta-amyloid proteins build first in the areas of the brain that support learning and memory. Physical evidence shows that the hippocampus is affected first, and then the disease spreads throughout the cerebral cortex. As the disease advances, symp-toms become more numerous and severe, including memory loss; disorientation; mood and behavior changes; confusion about events, time, and place; unfounded suspicions about family, friends, and caregivers; and finally, difficulty speaking, swallowing, and walking.

Although current Alzheimer's treatments can't stop the disease from progressing, they may temporarily slow the symp-toms. People with Alzheimer's live an average of eight years after symptoms become noticeable, depending on their age at diagnosis and other health problems they have.

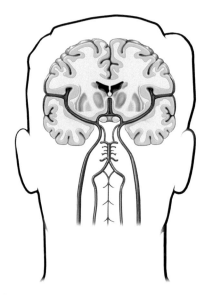

Blood supply
to the brain

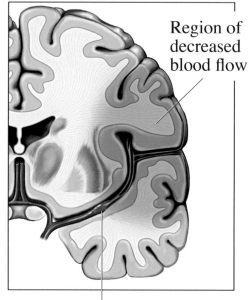

Region of
decreased
blood flow

Interruption of blood supply

If an interruption to the blood supply to the brain is corrected, the damage to the brain may be minimal. People should recognize the signs of a stroke and seek immediate medical attention.

Vascular Dementia

Vascular dementia is dementia that results from the interrupted flow of blood to the brain. The disrupted blood flow is called a stroke. When blood vessels to the brain are blocked, the lack of oxygen destroys brain cells. If enough brain cells die, a person's memory, speech, or other body functions become damaged. Vascular dementia can also occur when blood vessels narrow or are torn. High cholesterol levels and high blood pressure are two leading risk factors for stroke.

This kind of dementia is the second-most common cause of memory loss. As with Alzheimer's disease, people with vascular dementia may experience confusion, depression, and an inability to organize thoughts. Other symptoms are unsteady walking, poor concentration, and a tendency to wander at night. Symptoms are connected to the part of the brain that was deprived of blood.

Although a serious stroke can lead to a sudden case of dementia, vascular dementia may also occur gradually through a series of mini-strokes (multi-infarct dementia). The dementia may stabilize with the prevention of further strokes. However, vascular dementia commonly occurs simultaneously with Alzheimer's disease.

Lewy Body Dementia

Lewy body dementia (or dementia with Lewy bodies) is a disorder named for the smooth, round protein lumps called alpha-synucleins, or Lewy bodies. Lewy bodies grow within neurons throughout the cerebral cortex and brain stem. The increase in Lewy bodies throughout these parts of the brain exhibits itself first as typical dementia symptoms of memory loss and disorganized speech but progresses into motor control problems such as balance problems and frequent falls. Other indications of Lewy body dementia are periods of staring, acting out dreams when asleep, and repeated hallucinations.

Frontotemporal Dementia

Frontotemporal dementia affects the frontal and temporal lobes of the brain. As the centers of personality, behavior, and language shrink, patients undergo personality changes, display inappropriate behavior, lack normal emotional response, and lose the ability to use and understand language. They may repeat a phrase over and over again without recognition of this behavior. More rarely, motor control is affected as well.

In a type of frontotemporal dementia called Pick's disease, tau proteins within neurons of the central nervous system malfunction and cause the neurons to swell. This type of dementia is difficult for doctors to diagnosis because it initially appears as mental illness.

Other Dementia-Causing Brain Disorders

Other brain disorders have been found to cause dementia in small percentages of patients. Huntington's disease is a hereditary disorder that lowers neurotransmitter levels and kills neurons that control voluntary movement and those in the cerebral cortex. It demonstrates itself in uncontrollable or jerking movements; fixed facial expressions, such as grimaces; changes in personality and behavior; and eventually, widespread mental and cognitive decline. Huntingtin is a protein that is found in both normal people and those with this disease.

Delirium and Dementia

Delirium and dementia are often mistaken for each other. Delirium is an unexpected occurrence of symptoms, including hallucinations, slurred speech, restlessness, and difficulty thinking. In order to make a diagnosis of dementia, delirium must be ruled out first. Delirium's sudden appearance is a signal of its presence, as well as its fluctuating levels of symptoms. People with dementia are more likely to experience delirium when they are ill. Unlike most types of dementia, delirium is treatable. If the illness, disorder, or medication causing the delirium is treated, its symptoms should disappear.

People with the disease have a genetic mutation that causes Huntingtin to behave differently. This illness takes hold earlier than Alzheimer's—between thirty and forty years of age—and may slowly progress over twenty years. Unfortunately, the disease can become more severe as it is passed through families, and it can affect other family members at even younger ages.

Creutzfeldt-Jakob disease is a very rare disease caused by prions (tiny infectious particles) that can be associated with dementia. Patients may develop symptoms such as speech impairment, lack of coordination, hallucinations, and personality changes. Unlike most dementias, these alterations happen over a matter of weeks. Death usually occurs in under a year. However, only about one in every million people contract this disorder.

MYTHS AND FACTS

Myth: People with dementia should not interact with others.

Fact: Social activities improve dementia sufferers' quality of life. In fact, socializing seems to lessen the likelihood of developing dementia at all.

Myth: People who remember details of their past cannot have dementia.

Fact: Some brain disorders that cause dementia affect a person's ability to retain newly learned information and recent memories first. Memories of the distant past may be accessed for some time.

Myth: Exercise has no effect on brain function.

Fact: Studies have found a link between moderate exercise and a reduced risk of dementia.

Dementia pugilistica—or boxer's syndrome—is found in people who have had recurring head injuries. The "tangle" proteins associated with Alzheimer's disease appear to develop due to repeated brain trauma, bringing about the early onset of symptoms nearly identical to Alzheimer's. The condition is not only

The involvement of family members during the treatment and diagnosis of dementia and its related diseases and disorders is important for support.

relevant to boxing but to any sport with physical content, such as football or hockey.

Dementia related to AIDS (acquired immunodeficiency syndrome) occurs in later stages of the disease. It probably stems from HIV (human immunodeficiency virus) itself, rather than an opportunistic infection, such as a fungus in the brain. Symptoms are commonly related to cognitive, behavior, and motor control problems. Current HIV medications have helped cut down the occurrence of AIDS-related dementia to 10 to 20 percent of those with AIDS.

Other disorders that affect movement, such as Parkinson's disease and multiple sclerosis, can lead to dementia. However, little is known about these links.

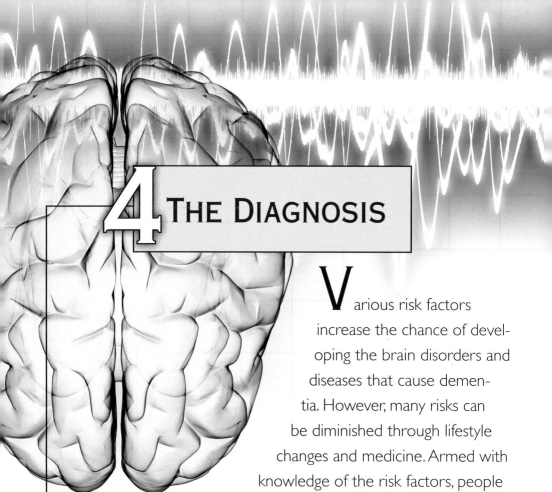

4 THE DIAGNOSIS

Various risk factors
increase the chance of developing the brain disorders and
diseases that cause dementia. However, many risks can
be diminished through lifestyle
changes and medicine. Armed with
knowledge of the risk factors, people
can better determine how to work
with their doctors for the treatment—or even
prevention—of dementia and its symptoms.

Risks: Uncontrollable and Controllable

Two uncontrollable contributing factors of dementia and its
disorders are age and family history. Alzheimer's disease, vascular dementia, and several other brain disorders are more
likely to occur at advanced ages. According to the Alzheimer's
Association, the probability of developing Alzheimer's doubles

about every five years after the age of sixty-five. After the age of eighty-five, the risk reaches nearly 50 percent.

People with relatives who have dementia are more likely to develop it, though family history does not guarantee an outcome. Brain disorders that result from genetic mutations—such as Huntington's disease—are passed down through families. Most doctors believe that genes alone do not cause dementia but that genes collaborate with other risk factors.

However, many factors in developing dementia can be controlled. To reduce the risk of dementia, the following should be addressed:

- **Alcohol use:** People who consume large amounts of alcohol are at more risk of developing dementia.

- **Blood pressure:** Blood pressure is the force of blood pushing against the walls of arteries. High blood pressure can damage and weaken blood vessels over the years, leading to stroke and vascular dementia. Extremely low blood pressure has been linked to Alzheimer's disease. Healthy lifestyle habits and medicines can help manage blood pressure.

- **Cholesterol:** Cholesterol accumulating on the walls of arteries leads to atherosclerosis. The buildup may eventually stop or slow blood flow to the brain, leading to stroke, vascular dementia, and possibly Alzheimer's disease. Unhealthy cholesterol can be lowered with exercise, a low-fat diet, and medicine.

• **Depression:** Depression and Alzheimer's are closely linked. Depression includes loss of interest in activities, changes in weight, sleeping difficulties, energy loss, and feelings of sadness and worthlessness. Studies show that depression in the elderly indicates the onset of Alzheimer's, and it may even be a contributing risk factor. There are effective treatments for depression, including medications.

• **Diabetes:** Diabetes is a disease characterized by high levels of blood glucose. In type 1 diabetes, the body does not make insulin (the hormone that helps glucose supply cells with energy), while in type 2 diabetes, the body does not respond to insulin. In time, this condition increases risk of both vascular dementia and Alzheimer's. Exercise, weight control, and medicine can help control diabetes.

People with diabetes, both young and old, need to take care of themselves to reduce the risk of developing dementia-related disorders.

- **Homocysteine:** High levels of an amino acid called homocysteine increase the risk of Alzheimer's disease and vascular dementia. Evidence suggests that homocysteine causes blood vessel damage and may disrupt neurotransmitters. This amino acid is broken down by vitamins B6, B12, and folic acid; a dietary deficiency of these should be corrected.

- **Smoking:** Smoking increases the risk of atherosclerosis and other vascular diseases that lead to dementia-related disorders. Heavy smoking may as much as double the risk of Alzheimer's later in life.

Determining a Diagnosis

People who experience the symptoms of dementia—or who think loved ones are experiencing them—should seek medical assistance. Diagnosis and immediate treatment may slow the advancement of dementia symptoms or even halt them altogether. The family doctor may refer the patient to a specialist, such as a neurologist, who focuses on the brain and nervous system.

Patients and caregivers should prepare for the appointment. If the patient does not yet have a caregiver, a friend or family member can offer support and add information about the patient's life. In addition, a support person can ask the doctor questions and record information.

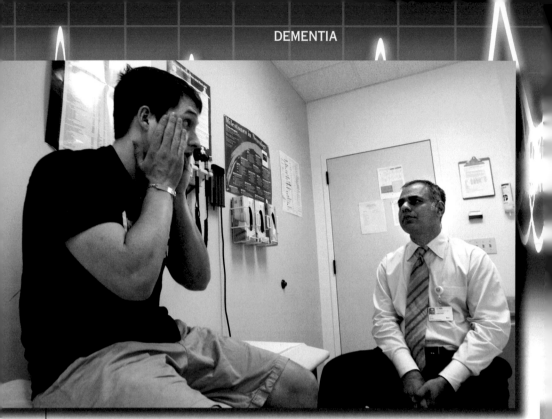

Friends or family members can help determine a diagnosis for someone with the signs of dementia by supplying doctors with as much personal and medical information as possible.

Patients should make notes of their medical history and current medications, vitamins, or supplements. The doctor will mostly likely ask a series of questions to determine diagnosis. These include:

- What symptoms are you experiencing?
- When did the symptoms begin?
- How severe are the symptoms?
- When do the symptoms appear or disappear?
- Have you experienced any head trauma?

The Mini-Mental State Exam

The Mini-Mental State Exam (MMSE), sometimes called the Mini-Mental Status Exam, is a screening test for dementia-related disorders. It tests various brain functions in about ten minutes, including spatial orientation, short-term memorization, ability to follow instructions, and object recognition. The test scores range from 0 to 30. The higher the score, the better the mental ability. Scores above 25 are labeled as normal. Scores between 10 and 20 signal that medical treatment is needed, while scores below 10 imply that the patient's condition may be beyond treatment. Besides an initial screening method, the MMSE is also used to measure cognitive decline over time. Many Alzheimer's patients score 3 to 4 points lower each year without treatment.

- Have there been any recent changes to medications being taken?
- Is there a family history of dementia or dementia-related disorders?
- How has your life changed so far because of the symptoms?

After the patient's medical history is examined, he or she will undergo a physical exam of overall health. Another round of tests checks balance and reflexes for problems in the nervous system.

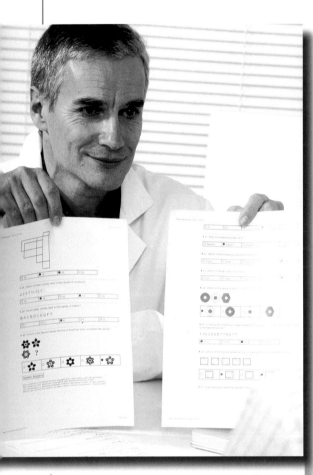

Several tests have been developed to detect and measure cognitive decline. A patient may take more than one as his or her doctor tries to determine a diagnosis of dementia or a related disorder.

Cognitive screening tests track language and spatial orientation, as well as concentration, memory, reasoning, and judgment. Two common evaluations are the MMSE and the Clinical Dementia Rating (CDR) scale. These tests not only aid in diagnosis; they also measure the degree of cognitive impairment and allow the physician to compare the decline of the patient over time. Parts of these evaluations include testing the patient's memory and attention by asking him or her to count backward and reciting words he or she has been told to remember.

The patient may be asked to smell several items and identify them. The plaques associated with memory loss in Alzheimer's disease build first in frontal areas of the brain, where neural processes of smell take place. Loss of smell is an indication of the onset of the disorder. These tests and others let doctors investigate if and what kind of dementia is present. However, they still fail to address the full spectrum of dementia symptoms, such as differences in mood, behavior, and personality.

Next, physical proof is sought in brain scans that can detect strokes, tumors, head injuries, and the buildup of fluid in the brain—all of which may result in dementia.

- **A CT or CAT (computerized axial tomography) scan** provides pictures of the brain by means of X-rays and a computer. Each X-ray captures a "slice" of the brain. When shown together, the entire brain structure can be examined.

- **An MRI (magnetic resonance imaging) scan** creates an image of the brain using radio signals produced by the body in response to magnets. While more time-consuming and expensive than CT, MRI allows the doctor to view the brain in much greater detail. Both CT and MRI, in conjunction with a dye, can help evaluate and detect blockages in the blood vessels that nourish the brain.

- **A PET (positron emission tomography) scan** with an injected radioactive dye can diagnose plaques in the brain associated with Alzheimer's. The dye binds to the plaques, revealing infected neurons in a three-dimensional image. Before this technology, plaques could be seen only in an autopsy. PET scans can also help distinguish Alzheimer's from other kinds of brain disorders.

- **An EEG (electroencephalogram)** uses devices attached to the head to measure and record electrical activity in the brain. This test has seen positive results in identifying those who will suffer from dementia in the future and those who will age normally.

There are many more laboratory tests used to diagnose dementia. Blood tests detect genes for dementia-causing disorders, and they check hormone levels and vitamin deficiencies. Urine tests measure levels of glucose and proteins, searching for abnormalities that may be addressed through nutrition or medication. Spinal fluid may reveal abnormal proteins that result from Alzheimer's disease.

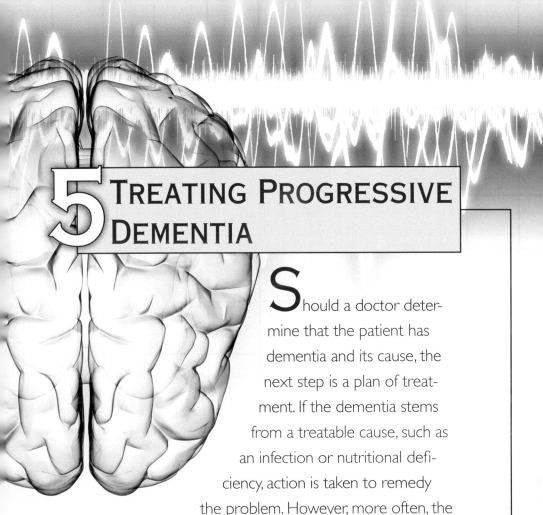

5 TREATING PROGRESSIVE DEMENTIA

Should a doctor determine that the patient has dementia and its cause, the next step is a plan of treatment. If the dementia stems from a treatable cause, such as an infection or nutritional deficiency, action is taken to remedy the problem. However, more often, the source of the problem is an untreatable brain disorder, such as Alzheimer's disease. Though there is no way to stop or reverse dementia in this case, there are medicines that have been developed to slow dementia's progression. Medication can also ease several symptoms associated with dementia.

Treating Alzheimer's Disease

One class of drugs commonly used to combat Alzheimer's disease is cholinesterase inhibitors. They slow the breakdown of

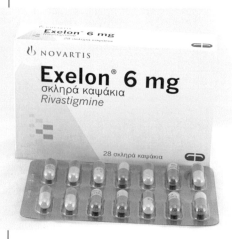

Though the medication rivastigmine doesn't slow the progression of Alzheimer's disease, it's a cholinesterase inhibitor that has been shown to improve cognitive functioning.

acetylcholine, a neurotransmitter that is deficient in the brains of people with Alzheimer's. Acetylcholine is a chemical that aids in the formation of memories. Studies have found that cholinesterase inhibitors halt the signs of dementia for a time and slow the progression of symptoms, including behavioral changes.

Another drug, memantine, regulates the neurotransmitter glutamate, which helps the neural processes of learning and remembering. Memantine is thought to work well in conjunction with cholinesterase inhibitors.

In addition to taking these medications, people in the early stages of Alzheimer's-related dementia should combat memory loss by using memory aids, such as lists and diaries.

Treating Vascular Dementia

There is no single course of action for treating vascular dementia. Some studies suggest that the same drugs offered to Alzheimer's patients are helpful in improving cognitive function and behavior problems in those with vascular dementia. However, prevention is most important. To prevent strokes,

Early-Onset Alzheimer's

Although Alzheimer's disease is typically thought of as an older person's affliction, it can affect people under sixty-five years old. Up to 5 percent of people diagnosed with Alzheimer's have what is termed "early-onset Alzheimer's." Many of these people are in their forties and fifties. Doctors are not sure why Alzheimer's affects these people at a younger age. However, those with early-onset Alzheimer's disease face a different set of difficulties than the elderly. They may have to learn how to deal with young families and their work lives, as well as their diagnoses.

doctors suggest lifestyle changes to combat high blood pressure, high cholesterol, heart disease, and diabetes. Medication may be necessary as well. A proper diet and regular exercise are the most effective ways of preventing and battling these conditions. Surgery may be necessary to increase blood supply to the brain.

Treating Other Brain Disorders

Cholinesterase inhibitors may also help reduce symptoms of dementia that coincide with Parkinson's disease. At this time, no medications are thought to help with frontotemporal dementia, Lewy body dementia, or Creutzfeldt-Jakob disease. However, symptoms that accompany the dementia, such as depression, tremors, and pain, can be treated.

10 GREAT QUESTIONS
TO ASK A DOCTOR

1. What are the most common symptoms of dementia?
2. What are the most common causes of dementia?
3. What kinds of tests for dementia are necessary?
4. What is the best course of action for treating or managing dementia?
5. What are the side effects of treatment?
6. Are there alternative plans of treatment for dementia?
7. Should multiple doctors or specialists be consulted?
8. Is dementia treatment typically covered under health insurance?
9. How should I change my lifestyle to prevent dementia?
10. What books, Web sites, or other materials will help best explain dementia?

Alternative Medicines

Some people choose to combat dementia with vitamins and herbal supplements.

Vitamin E is an antioxidant acquired largely through diet. (For example, fish, vegetable oils, and green vegetables contain vitamin E.) Antioxidants prevent the destruction of neurons and other cells. One study suggests that vitamin E delays, but does not improve, dementia symptoms.

Omega-3 fatty acids are found in foods such as fish and nuts. They benefit the heart and blood vessels, as well as support and protect neurons. Omega-3 fatty acids are also effective in fighting depression.

Coenzyme Q10 is an antioxidant made by the body and needed for basic cell function. Levels of coenzyme Q10 appear to diminish with aging. Though a man made version has been offered as a way to treat dementia, no study has proven that the substance alters symptoms. In high doses, it causes negative side effects such as low blood pressure and low blood sugar.

Vitamins B12, B6, and E, as well as folic acid, have been proposed to lower levels of the amino acid homocysteine. High levels of homocysteine signal the threat of Alzheimer's disease and vascular dementia. Doctors suggest that these vitamins be acquired through diet if possible, rather than vitamin supplements.

Gingko is an extract from the leaves of the gingko biloba tree. While some believe it can help with memory problems, most research studies have proven inconclusive. However, gingko has been found to have antioxidant properties.

Huperzine A is made from a plant called Chinese club moss. It is currently marketed as a memory booster after some research in animal studies suggested it improves memory function. It appears to work in ways similar to cholinesterase inhibitors.

As with any medication, alternative medicines, vitamins, and supplements should be taken under the care of a doctor to prevent unwanted side effects and overdoses. It is important that the doctor be aware of all alternative medications, as sometimes they may interact with medications the doctor prescribes and can lead to harmful consequences. Many of the studies undertaken for some alternative medicines support the fact that a healthy diet, as well as regular exercise, reduces the risk of dementia.

Omega-3 fatty acids, an important part of a healthy diet, are found in foods such as walnuts, olive oil, salmon, flax seeds, and some eggs.

Breakthroughs in Medicine

Many recent studies point to breakthroughs on the horizon for treatment of dementia and related brain disorders. Scientists have found the genes that are involved in Alzheimer's development. They have separated them into two categories: genes that increase the likelihood of developing the disease, and genes that guarantee the disease will occur. The identification of these genes may lead to new drug treatments.

Extensive research is being done in labs around the world. About 90 percent of what is known about Alzheimer's has been discovered in the last fifteen years.

In addition, new developments in the early detection of Alzheimer's give hope to those diagnosed with the disease. Though there are still no medicines that can change the course of the disease, the drugs that are currently used seem to have a greater effect on those in the early stages of Alzheimer's. This means that a higher quality of life may be maintained for a longer amount of time than ever before.

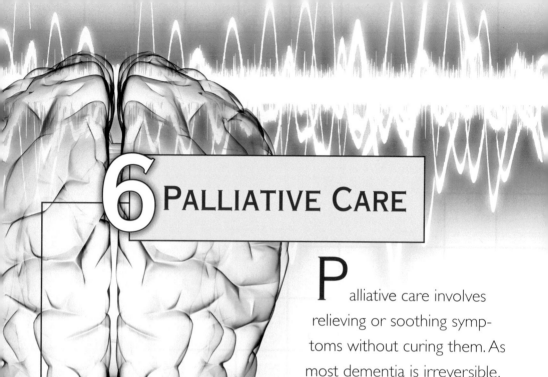

6 PALLIATIVE CARE

Palliative care involves relieving or soothing symptoms without curing them. As most dementia is irreversible, palliative care is of the utmost importance in keeping people with dementia as active and comfortable as possible. Perhaps the most important task after a dementia diagnosis is creating a plan for the future. Answering questions and tackling potential problems gives dementia patients a way to control their lives.

If patients are still living at home, they should find ways to make their home as safe as possible. Fixtures such as stairs and bathtubs can become difficult for people whose dementia affects their motor control. Most accidents happen in the kitchen and bathroom.

Patients should decide if they need home help, such as a nurse or aide, and how much time this professional should

Nursing homes and assisted-living facilities are two options for those with progressive dementia. Family members may find their loved ones need round-the-clock monitoring.

spend with them. They should also make decisions about the point at which they cannot live at home alone anymore or when care may become too difficult for their spouse. At this stage, should they move in with other family or into a nursing facility?

After creating a detailed plan of care, those diagnosed with dementia should do all they can to keep their life as normal, productive, and interesting as possible. There are several methods of combating further cognitive decline.

Exercising the Brain

People with dementia should keep their thought processes as active as possible. Many studies have found that people who frequently engage in cognitive activities—such as reading, solving puzzles, taking classes, or engaging in other thought-provoking activities—reduce their risk of developing dementia. The motto "Use it or lose it" appears to have truth behind it. Though continuing such activities after diagnosis cannot reverse the progress of dementia, cognitive stimulation may keep symptoms from becoming more severe.

Just as most people need to make lists to remind them of important tasks, those with dementia may find that even everyday tasks are escaping their memory. Multiple lists in easy-to-see places may become necessary.

In the early stages of memory loss, dementia patients should create lists to help them remember appointments, events, and tasks. As memory worsens, caregivers should create these lists and fill in calendars for the patients to check. Important phone numbers for emergencies should be clearly posted in many places throughout the home. Someone should call or visit daily to remind the patient of the day's activities, as well as to make sure that he or she is safe.

Coping with Emotions

Anger, grief, frustration, and hopelessness are the common emotions that come with a dementia diagnosis. They need to be addressed as much as any symptom of dementia itself. Depression has been shown to make symptoms progress further and faster. Support groups are available for the diagnosed to share their feelings and learn how others cope. Online support communities also exist. Journal writing is a more personal and private outlet for dealing with emotions.

Fulfilling Roles

According to studies reported in the medical journal *The Gerontologist*, asking patients with advanced dementia to give advice and teach leads to successful focus on activities. In one case, the patients were asked to counsel others on how to raise children. The patients were both alert and informative with their answers. In fact, they were much more easy to understand than when asked to provide information about their past lives. In another study, patients were given pictures to aid them in teaching a recipe. With some help, they completed the task effectively.

The results of these studies suggest that those with dementia thrive in roles they had when they were younger—those of parents, grandparents, teachers, and mentors.

Caregiving

At some point, a person suffering from dementia will not be able to clearly make his or her own decisions. Who will make the health care choices at that point? There are a lot of hard decisions to make after diagnosis, many of which involve legal and financial matters. So the person chosen to make these decisions should know the patient's wishes.

Caregiving for those with dementia usually falls on the shoulders of family and friends. Spouses, children, and other family members may choose to care for their loved one in their own home for a time. They may also have health care professionals help them.

Creating a regular pattern of activities for the patient each day can combat anxiety. Established rituals are especially helpful at night, when dementia often worsens due to disorientation from fatigue and the lack of light.

If dementia patients suffer from paranoia or hallucinations, several things may help ease their minds. First, arguing or reasoning rarely makes a difference. Keep calm in order to give a sense that nothing is wrong. However, rather than ignore their feelings, acknowledge them. Tell them it is understandable to be worried or frightened. In addition, having the same people around the patient is key to building trust.

If the dementia patient has difficulties understanding speech, keep sentences short. Avoid questions that may cause anxiety. Talk in a calm and even voice. Speak slowly and wait for a response. Use signals to help the person understand what is being said. It may be helpful for nonverbal patients to have a notepad to write questions and comments as well.

Sometimes when dementia patients are very confused and anxious about communicating, being affectionate is a good way to calm them. An arm around their shoulder or holding their hand can make a difference in mood. Studies suggest that even those with severe memory loss understand and are thankful for attention.

People with dementia can enjoy celebrations, events, or a walk outside on a beautiful day, just like anyone else. These times are important for fighting the depression associated with dementia as well.

Watching a loved one go through changes in personality, behavior, and cognitive ability is painful. Taking care of someone who no longer recognizes you or acts aggressively is even more heartbreaking. Caregivers need as much support as the diagnosed. There are support groups available for caregivers and families of those with dementia. Professionals and people who have experienced dementia within their families can offer advice on how to handle difficult situations. Above all, caretakers must take care of themselves. At some point, it may be essential to the patient's safety to hire another person to help or to move into a nursing facility.

Hope for the Future

Adopting an optimistic attitude about the future may seem impossible when faced with the diagnosis of dementia. However, there is reason to hope. Thousands of researchers are probing for new ways to halt and cure the disorders that cause dementia. Remember, most of what we know about dementia and related brain disorders has been discovered in the past decade. We have valuable knowledge about what we can do to prevent dementia with diet and exercise. What will the next decade bring? In the meantime, we can strive to give those with dementia the most meaningful, enjoyable, and pain-free life possible.

Glossary

amino acid The building block that makes up proteins and is important to living cells.

anesthesia A drug used to make the body insensitive to pain.

antioxidant A substance that stops the destructive effects that oxygen can have in the body.

atherosclerosis A disease in which cholesterol deposits form within arteries.

autopsy A medical exam of a human cadaver.

cholesterol A fatlike substance found in animal tissue, blood, eggs, and fats.

cognitive Describing the process of acquiring knowledge.

deficiency A lack or shortage of something.

diagnosis The identifying of an illness or disorder in a patient.

hallucination The perception of somebody or something that is not really there.

leukemia A type of cancer in which white blood cells replace normal blood cells.

limbic system A group of brain structures associated with smell, emotion, behavior, and various automatic functions.

malnutrition A lack of healthy foods in the diet.

membrane A thin layer of tissue.

multiple sclerosis A disease of the nervous system.

neurodegenerative Causing a loss of structure or function in nerve cells, their connections, or supportive tissue.

onset The beginning of something.

paranoia Unreasonable feelings of suspicion.

spatial orientation A sense of direction while moving around an environment.

supplement A substance with a nutritional value added to the diet.

trauma An extremely distressing experience or a physical injury.

For More Information

Alzheimer's Association

919 N. Michigan Avenue, Floor 17

Chicago, IL 60601

(800) 272-3900

Web site: http://www.alz.org

The Alzheimer's Association provides news on the latest research, tips about caring for those with the disease, and message boards to exchange information.

Alzheimer Society of Canada

20 Eglinton Avenue West, Suite 1600

Toronto, ON M4R 1K8

Canada

(416) 488-8772

Web site: http://www.alzheimer.ca

This organization provides information about Alzheimer's research and ways to seek help in Canada.

ARCH National Respite Network and Resource Center

800 Eastowne Drive, Suite 105

Chapel Hill, NC 27514

(919) 490-5577

Web site: http://www.archrespite.org

Respite care assists families under stress due to caring for an ill loved one.

This center finds those seeking help services in their communities.

Lewy Body Dementia Association (LBDA)

912 Killian Hill Road SW

Lilburn, GA 30047

(404) 935-6444

Web site: http://www.lbda.org

LBDA focuses on support and information for Lewy body dementia sufferers and caregivers.

National Institute of Mental Health (NIMH)

6001 Executive Boulevard

Room 8184 MSC 9663

Bethesda, MD 20892-9663

(866) 615-6464

Web site: http://www.nimh.nih.gov

NIMH seeks to understand and treat mental illnesses through research. Its site provides information on all kinds of mental health issues.

National Institute of Neurological Disorders and Stroke (NINDS)

National Institutes of Health

P.O. Box 5801

Bethesda, MD 20824

(800) 352-9424

Web site: http://www.ninds.nih.gov

NINDS seeks to prevent and treat the disorders that affect the nervous system.

National Institute on Aging (NIA)

Building 31, Room 5C27

31 Center Drive, MSC 2292

Bethesda, MD 20892

(301) 496-1752

Web site: http://www.nia.nih.gov

NIA supports research related to aging and the diseases and conditions that result from that process.

Neurological Health Charities Canada

c/o Parkinson Society Canada

4211 Yonge Street, Suite 316

Toronto, ON M2P 2A9

Canada

(800) 565-3000

Web site: http://www.mybrainmatters.ca

Neurological Health Charities is a group of organizations that represent Canadians with progressive neurological diseases and disorders.

Web Sites

Due to the changing nature of Internet links, Rosen Publishing has developed an online list of Web sites related to the subject of this book. This site is updated regularly. Please use this link to access the list:

http://www.rosenlinks.com/bdis/deme

For Further Reading

Ballenger, Jesse. *Treating Dementia: Do We Have a Pill for It?*
Baltimore, MD: Johns Hopkins University Press, 2009.

Beaumont, Helen. *Losing Clive to Younger Onset Dementia: One
Family's Story.* Philadelphia, PA: Jessica Kingsley, 2009.

Bonner, Dede. *The 10 Best Questions for Living with Alzheimer's:
The Script You Need to Take Control of Your Health.* New York,
NY: Simon & Schuster, 2008.

Carper, Jean. *100 Simple Things You Can Do to Prevent Alzheimer's
and Age-Related Memory Loss.* New York, NY: Little, Brown
and Company, 2010.

Dezell, Maureen, and Carrie Hill. *The Everything Guide to
Alzheimer's Disease: A Reassuring, Informative Guide for
Families and Caregivers.* Avon, MA: Adams Media, 2009.

Genova, Lisa. *Still Alice: A Novel.* New York, NY: Pocket
Books, 2009.

Gibbons, Leeza, James Huysman, and Rosemary DeAngelis
Laird. *Take Your Oxygen First: Protecting Your Health and
Happiness While Caring for a Loved One with Memory Loss.*
New York, NY: Lachance Publishing, 2009.

Goethe, Katherine E., and Martha E. Leatherman. *The Insider's
Guide to Dementia Care: What You Should Know About
Assisted Living, Alzheimer's, and Dementia Care.* Livermore,
CA: WingSpan Press, 2009.

Hardman, Lizabeth. *Dementia.* Detroit, MI: Lucent Books, 2009.

Hodges, John. *Frontotemporal Dementia Syndromes.* New York,
NY: Cambridge University Press, 2007.

James, Oliver. *Contented Dementia*. London, England: Vermilion, 2009.

James, Vaughn E. *The Alzheimer's Advisor: A Caregiver's Guide to Dealing with the Tough Legal and Practical Issues*. New York, NY: American Management Association, 2009.

Mace, Nancy L., and Peter V. Rabins. *The 36-Hour Day: A Family Guide to Caring for People with Alzheimer's Disease, Other Dementias, and Memory Loss in Later Life*. Baltimore, MD: Johns Hopkins University Press, 2006.

Mosley, Walter. *The Last Days of Ptolemy Grey*. New York, NY: Riverhead Books, 2010.

Pearce, Nancy D. *Inside Alzheimer's: How to Hear and Honor Connections with a Person Who Has Dementia*. Taylors, SC: Forrason Press, 2007.

Sabbagh, Marwan Noel. *The Alzheimer's Answer: Reduce Your Risk and Keep Your Brain Healthy*. Hoboken, NJ: Wiley, 2008.

Smith, William. *Exercise for Dementia: Complete Fitness Plan with Physical and Mental Exercises for Dementia Patients or Those at Risk for Dementia*. Long Island City, NY: Hatherleigh Press, 2009.

Whalley, Lawrence J., and John C. S. Breitner. *Fast Facts: Dementia*. Oxford, England: Health Press, 2009.

Whitman, Lucy. *Telling Tales About Dementia: Experiences of Caring*. Philadelphia, PA: Jessica Kingsley, 2009.

Index

A

acquired immunodeficiency syndrome (AIDS), 31
active roles, for dementia patients, 51–52
age, as uncontrollable factor of dementia, 32–33
alcohol addiction, 22, 23, 33
alternative treatments, 44–46
Alzheimer's disease, 5, 24–25, 27, 29, 30, 32–33, 34, 35, 37, 38, 39, 40, 45, 46
  early-onset Alzheimer's, 43
  treating, 41–42, 47
apraxia, 19

B

behavior changes, 5, 13, 16, 54
blood pressure, 26, 33, 43
brain stem, 11
brain tumors, 5, 24, 39
B vitamins, 22, 35

C

calcium, 22
caregiving, 14, 25, 35, 50, 52–54
cerebellum, 11
cerebral cortex, 7, 9, 10, 25, 27, 28
cerebrum, 6, 7–9, 11
cholesterol, 26, 33–34, 43
cognitive exercises, 50–51
communication problems, 13, 16–17
Creutzfeldt-Jakob disease, 29, 43
CT scan, 39

D

dehydration, 19, 22
delirium, 29
dementia pugilistica, 30–31
depression, 20, 22, 27, 34, 43, 51
diabetes, 34, 43
diagnosing dementia, 35–40, 52
drug addiction, 23

E

EEG, 40
encephalitis, 21
endocrine system, 22
executive dysfunction, 13, 14
exercise, 30, 34, 43, 46, 54

F

family history, as uncontrollable factor of dementia, 32, 33
forgetfulness (contrasted with dementia), 18
frontal lobe, 7–8, 9, 16, 28
frontotemporal dementia, 28, 43

H

hippocampus, 9
home help, 14, 48–49
homocysteine, 35, 45
human immunodeficiency virus (HIV), 31
Huntington's disease, 28–29, 33
hygiene, 19
hypoglycemia, 22
hypothyroidism, 22

I

infections, 21–22, 31, 41

J

journal writing, 51

L

leukemia, 22
Lewy body dementia, 27, 43
long-term memory, 9, 10, 30

M

malnutrition, 5, 19, 22, 41
medicine
  forgetting to take, 18–19
  for treating dementia, 32,
    41–47
  side effects that mimic
    dementia, 23
memory loss, 13–14, 18
meningitis, 22
Mini-Mental State Exam,
  37, 38
MRI scan, 39
multiple sclerosis, 22, 31

N

neurodegeneration, what it is, 12
nursing facilities, 49, 54

O

occipital lobe, 8
oxygen, 23, 26

P

parietal lobe, 8, 9, 10, 16
Parkinson's disease, 31, 43
personality changes, 5, 13, 16, 22,
    29, 54
PET scan, 39–40

S

short-term memory, 9–10, 14,
    22, 30
sleeping, 20
smoking, 35
social activities, 30
sodium, 22
spatial disorientation, 13, 15
subdural hematoma, 24
support groups, 51, 54

T

temporal lobe, 8, 10, 16, 28

V

vascular dementia, 26–27, 32, 33, 34,
    35, 45
  treating, 42–43
vitamin deficiencies, 22

About the Author

Therese Shea is the author of more than two hundred nonfiction books. She attended Providence College and the State University of New York at Buffalo, where she earned her master's in secondary education. She thanks her husband, Mark Harasymiw, MLS, JD, sister Mary Molly Shea, RN, MSN, and brother John Shea, MD, Ph.D. for their help in researching and writing this book. Shea currently resides in Atlanta, Georgia.

Photo Credits

Cover, back cover, and interior background images and elements (nerve cells, brain waves, brains) Shutterstock.com; p. 5 Jupiterimages/Photos.com/Thinkstock; p. 7 © www.istockphoto.com/Todd Harrison; p. 10 Thomas Northcut/Photodisc/Getty Images; p. 12 Ingram Publishing/Agency Collection/Getty Images; pp. 15, 19 iStockphoto/Thinkstock; p. 17 Hemera/Thinkstock; p. 23 CAVALLINI/Gamma-Rapho via Getty Images; p. 26 Nucleus Medical Art, Inc./Getty Images; p. 31 krtphotos/Newscom; p. 34 E. Jason Wambsgans/Chicago Tribune/MCT via Getty Images; p. 36 Lezlie Sterling/Sacramento Bee/MCT via Getty Images; p. 38 © BSIP/Photo Researchers, Inc.; p. 42 © SPL/Photo Researchers, Inc.; p. 46 Foodie Photography/FoodPix/Getty Images; p. 47. Waltraud Grubitzch/dpa/Landov; p. 49 Dann Tardif/LWA/Photographer's Choice/Getty Images; p. 50 Frank Siteman/Doctor Stock/Science Faction/Getty Images; p. 53 Comstock/Thinkstock.

Designer: Les Kanturek; Editor: Nicholas Croce;
Photo Researcher: Amy Feinberg

12/13